PIANO *for* TWO

DUETS EQUAL PARTS FOR ONE PIANO, 4 HANDS

arranged by
Carol Matz

Production: Frank and Gail Hackinson
Production Coordination and Text Design: Marilyn Cole
Editors: Victoria McArthur and Edwin McLean
Cover: Terpstra Design, San Francisco
Engraving: GrayBear Music Company, Hollywood, Florida
Printer: Tempo Music Press, Inc.

THE
F·J·H
MUSIC
COMPANY
INC.

Frank J. Hackinson

ISBN 1-56939-043-6

A Note to Teachers

Most students find duet playing to be a fun and challenging addition to their everyday piano studies. Duets offer students a chance to learn from the experience of making music with another person. **Piano for Two** provides a wonderful opportunity for students to work on aspects of ensemble playing, such as dynamic balance and tempo control, while learning some of their favorite well-known pieces.

In these arrangements, no eighth notes or dotted-quarter rhythms are used. Students will predominantly stay in five-finger position. When occasional movement outside the position occurs, circled finger numbers signal the position change.

For easier reading, one or both parts call for an octave transposition, which is clearly marked in the score. Additionally, the melodies often shift between *primo* and *secondo*, affording the opportunity to work on dynamic blending.

Piano for Two is available in six volumes, ranging in difficulty from early elementary through late intermediate/advanced levels. Students will be delighted by the variety of pieces included in each book, representing the classics, well-known favorites, original pieces, and more.

CONTENTS

When the Saints Go Marching In

Secondo

Traditional American

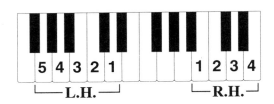

With spirit
(Play as written)

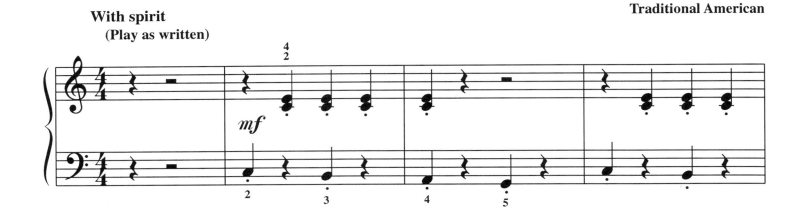

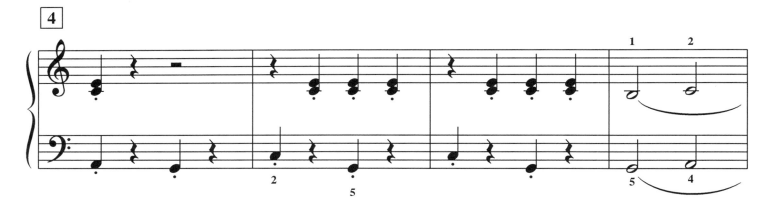

how I want to be in that num - ber,_____

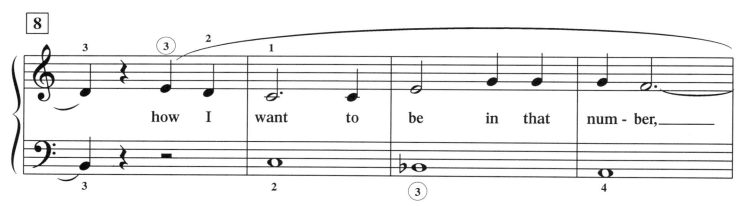

_____ when the saints go march - ing in.

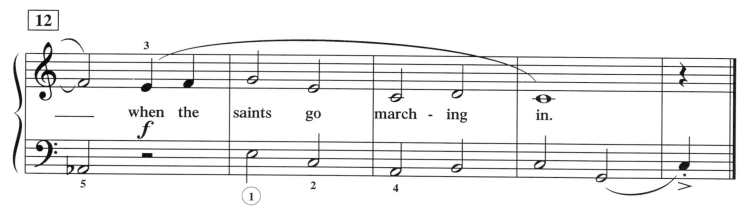

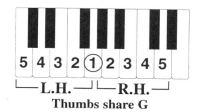

When the Saints Go Marching In

Primo

With spirit
(Play both hands 1 octave higher)

Traditional American

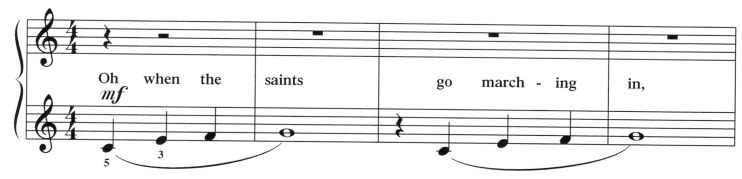

Oh when the saints go march - ing in,

mf

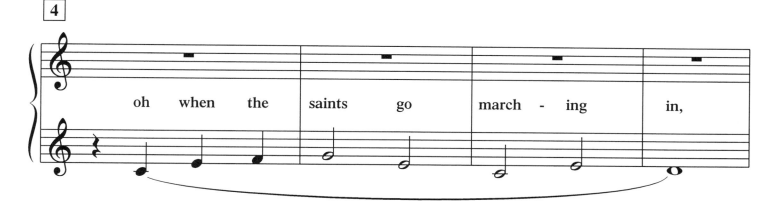

oh when the saints go march - ing in,

mp

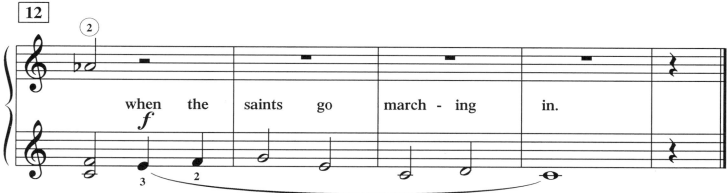

when the saints go march - ing in.

f

FF1145

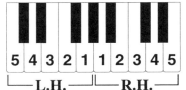

Ode to Joy

Secondo

Ludwig van Beethoven

FF1145

Ode to Joy

Primo

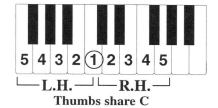

Ludwig van Beethoven

Moderately
(Play both hands 1 octave higher)

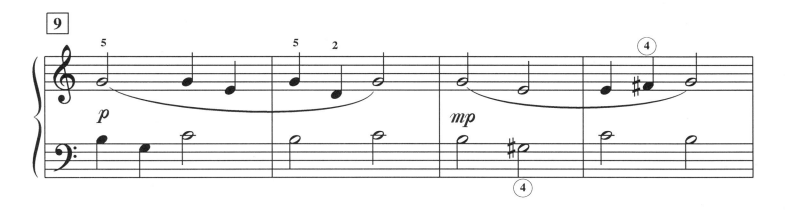

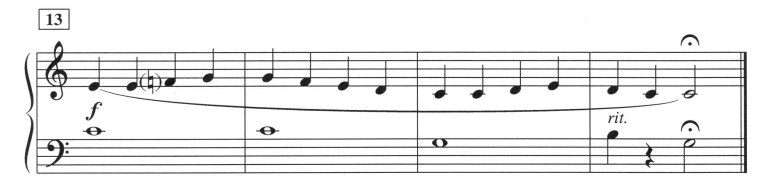

8

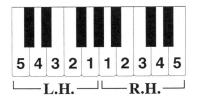

Irish Washerwoman

Secondo

Traditional Irish Jig

Happily
(Play as written)

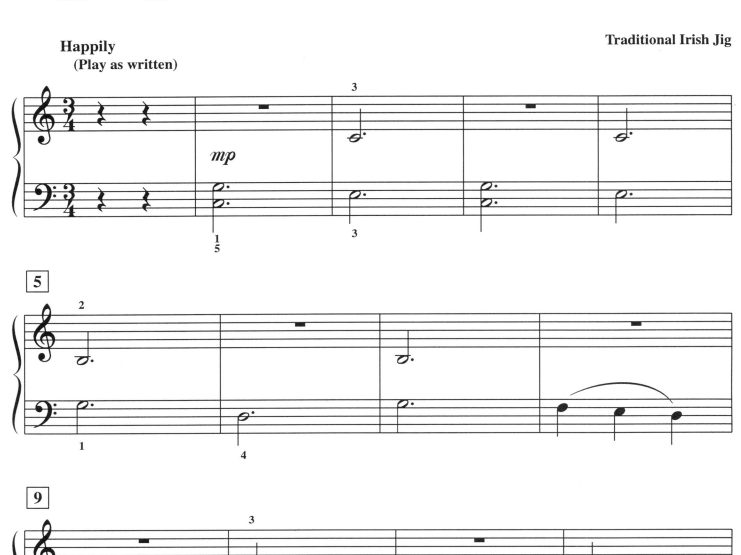

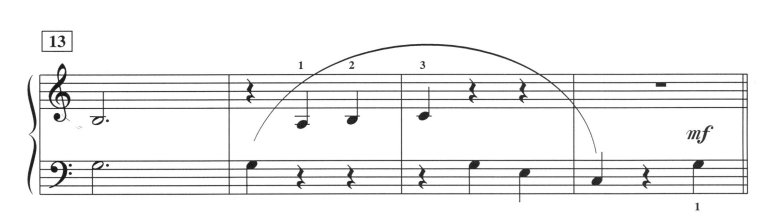

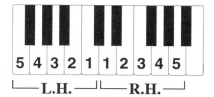

Irish Washerwoman

Primo

Happily
(Play both hands 1 octave higher)

Traditional Irish Jig

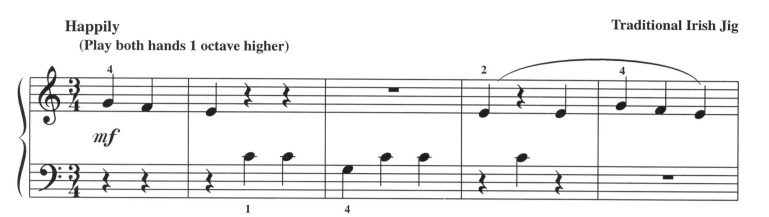

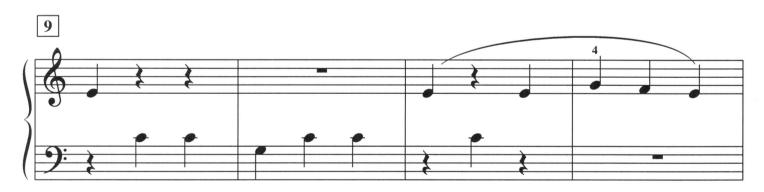

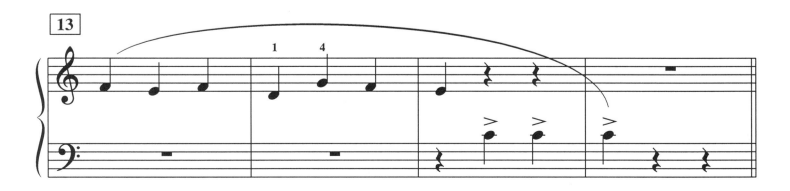

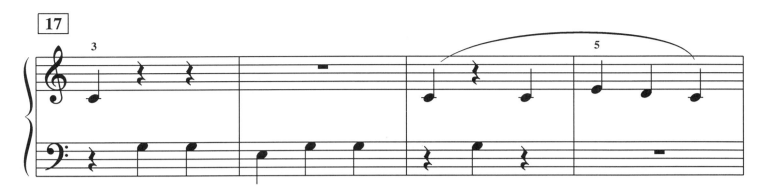

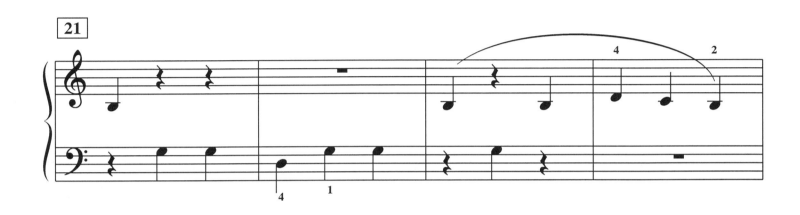

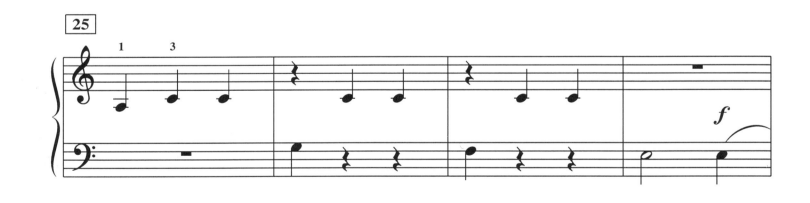

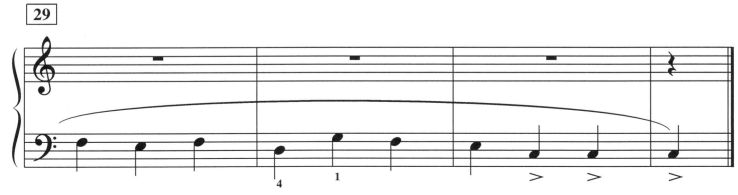

Primo

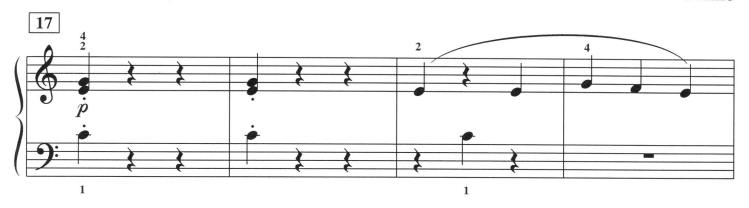

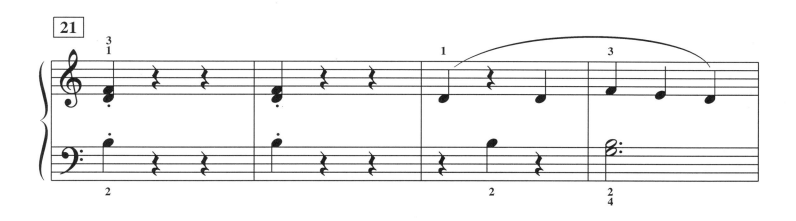

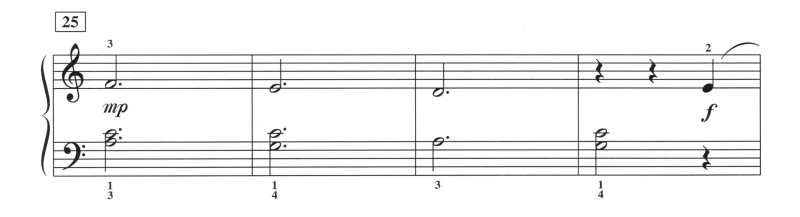

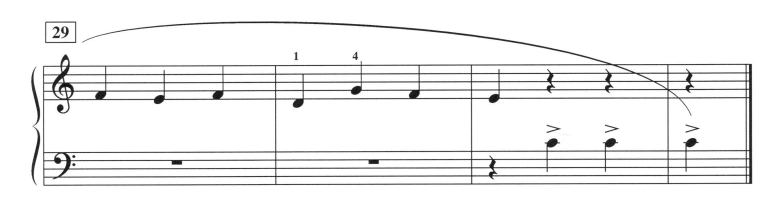

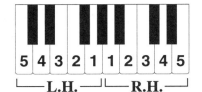

A Bicycle Built For Two
(Daisy Bell)
Secondo

Words and Music by
Harry Dacre

Flowing
(Play both hands 1 octave lower)

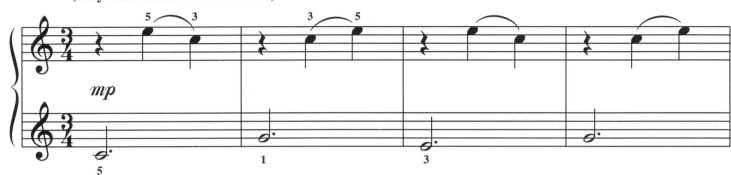

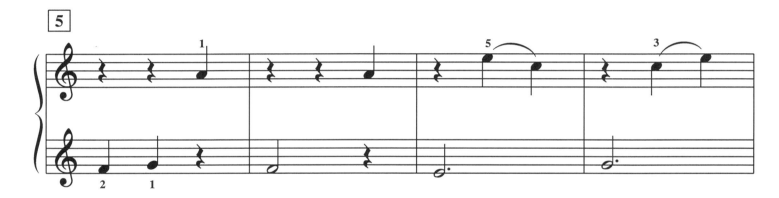

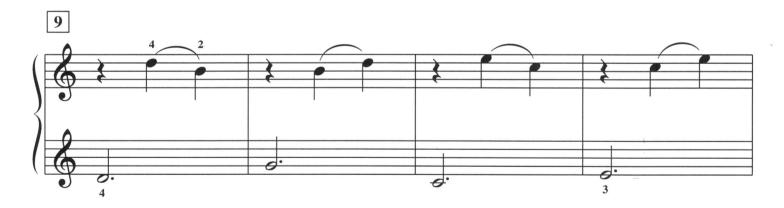

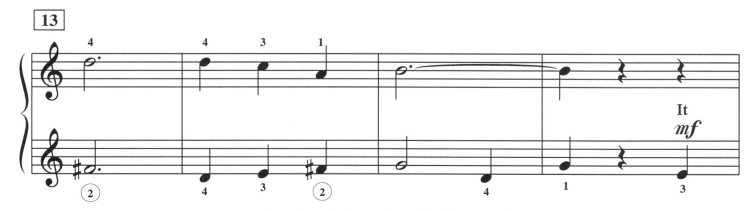

It

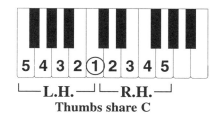

A Bicycle Built For Two
(Daisy Bell)

Primo

Words and Music by
Harry Dacre

Flowing
(Play both hands 1 octave higher)

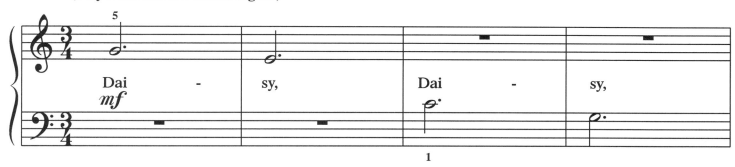

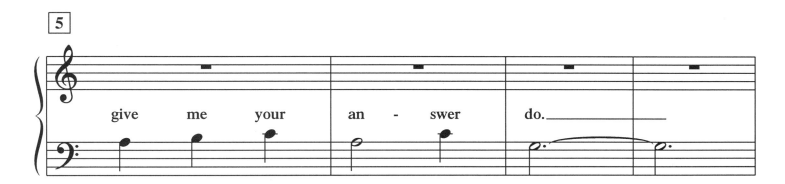

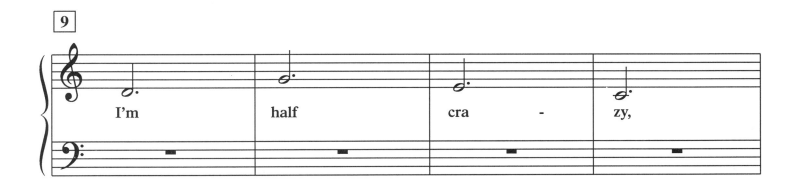

FF1145

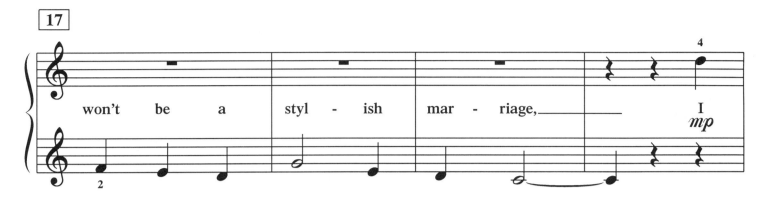

won't be a styl - ish mar - riage,_____ I

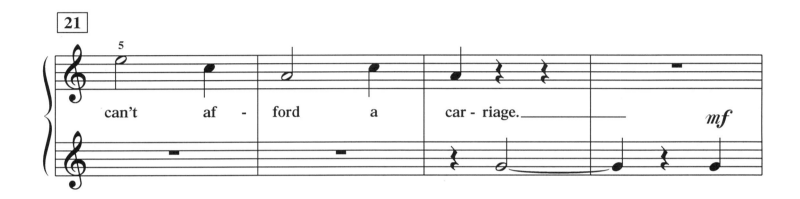

can't af - ford a car - riage._____

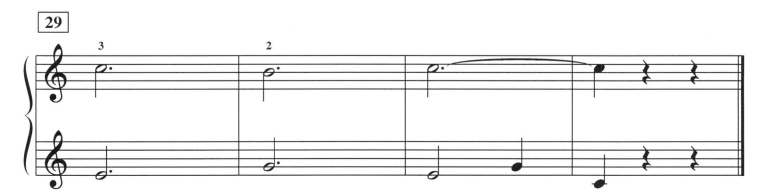

17

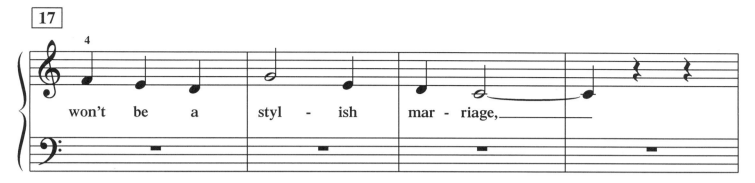

won't be a styl - ish mar - riage,____

21

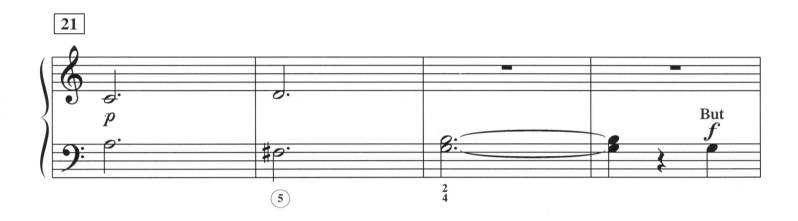

But

25

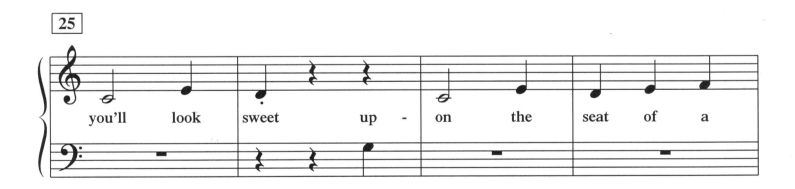

you'll look sweet up - on the seat of a

29

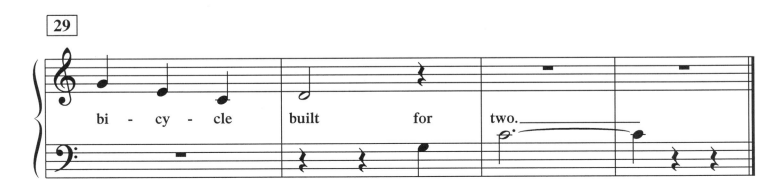

bi - cy - cle built for two.____

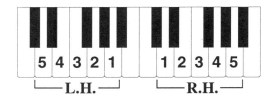

Russian Wedding Dance

Secondo

Carol Matz

Moderately fast
(Play both hands 1 octave lower)

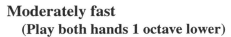

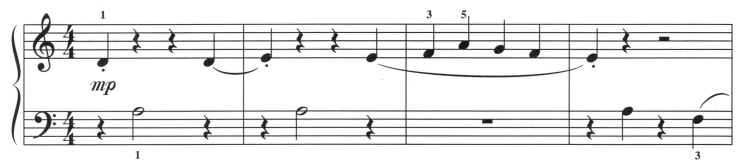

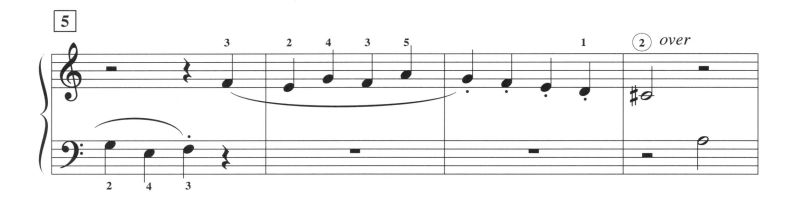

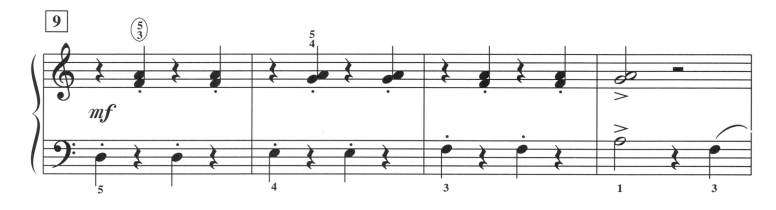

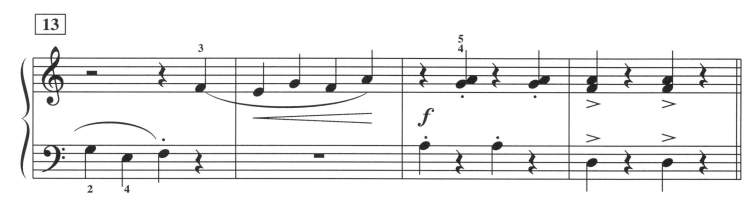

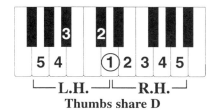

Russian Wedding Dance

Primo

Carol Matz

Moderately fast
(Play both hands 1 octave higher)

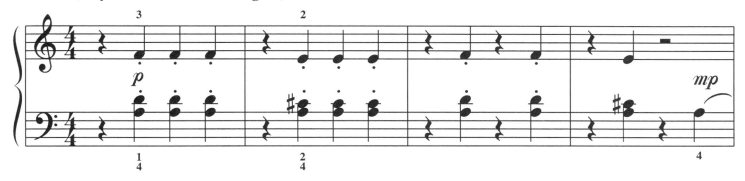

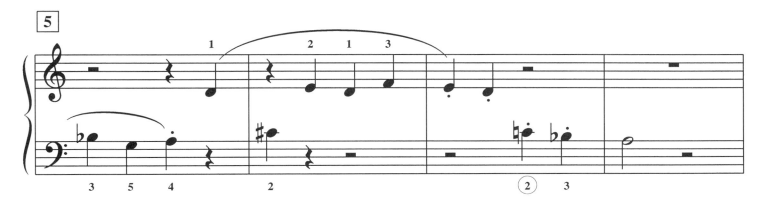

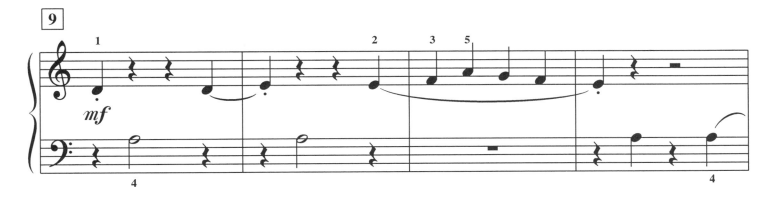

17

21
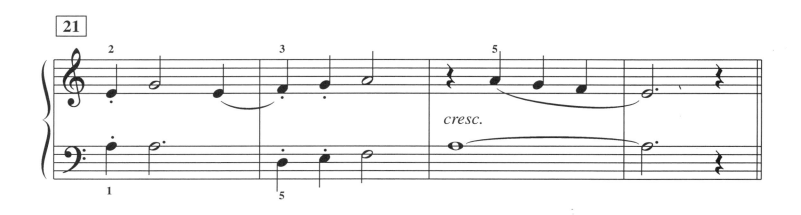

25
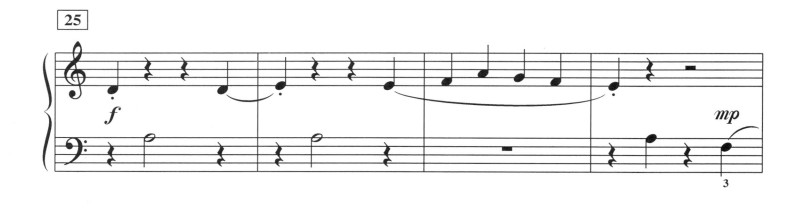

29
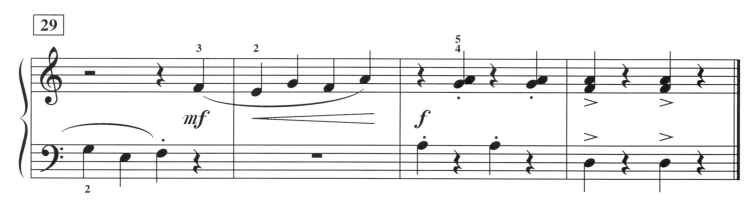

Primo

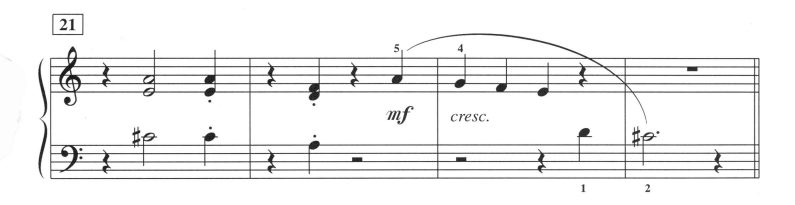

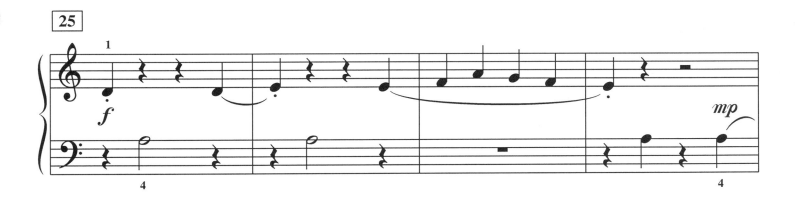

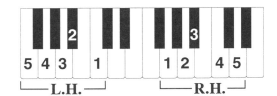

Take Me Out to the Ball Game

Secondo

Words by Jack Norworth
Music by Albert Von Tilzer

Moderate waltz tempo
(Play both hands 1 octave lower)

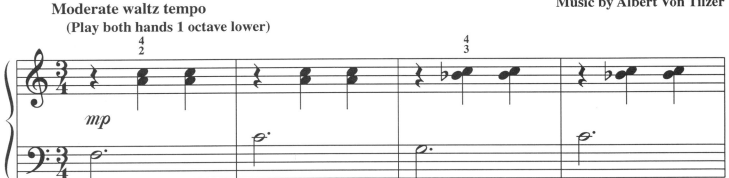

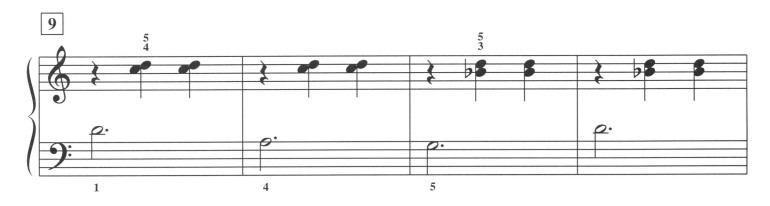

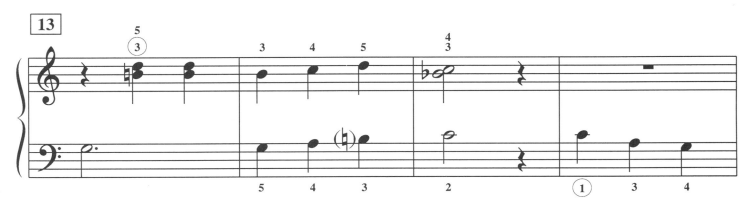

Take Me Out to the Ball Game

Primo

Words by Jack Norworth
Music by Albert Von Tilzer

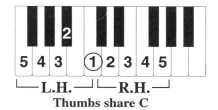

Moderate waltz tempo
(Play both hands 1 octave higher)

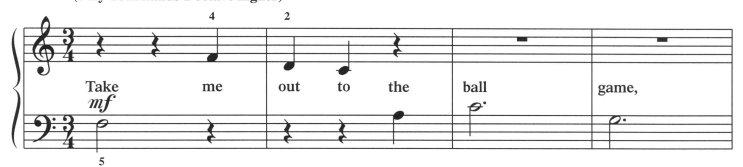

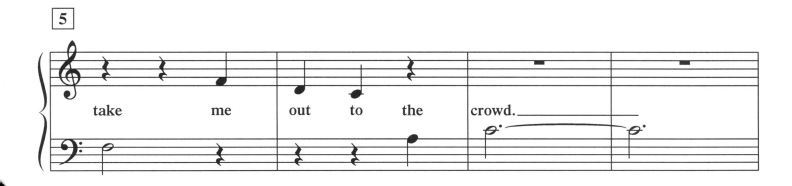

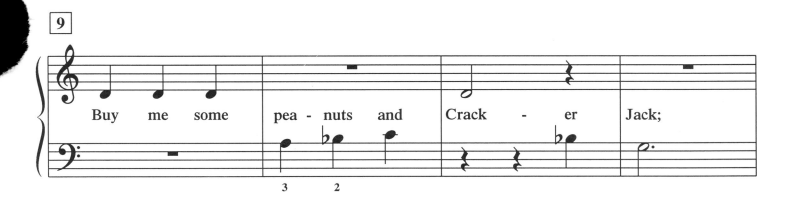

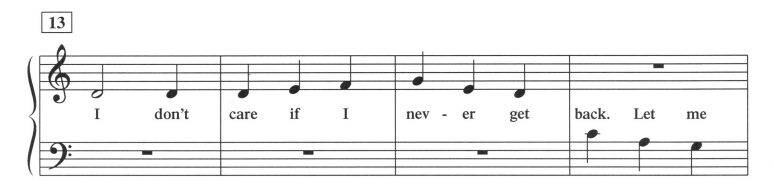

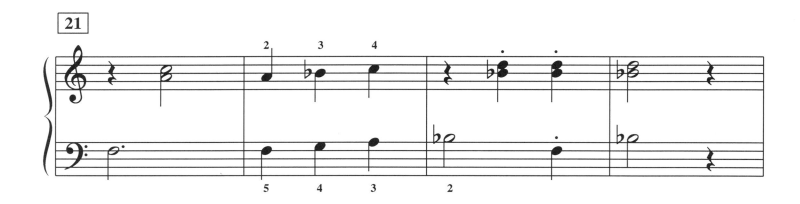

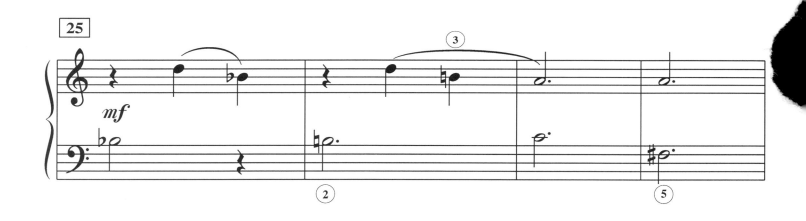

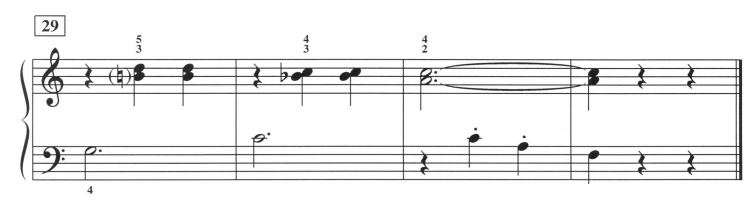

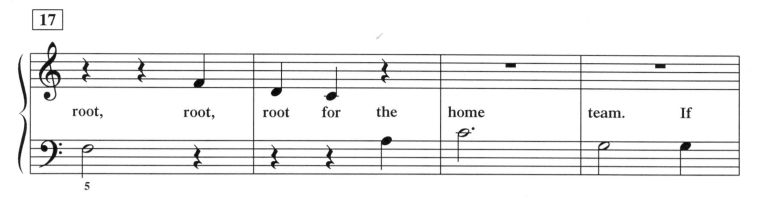

17

root,   root,   root for the   home   team.   If

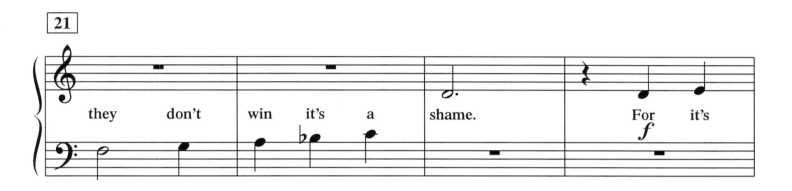

21

they   don't   win it's   a   shame.   For   it's
f

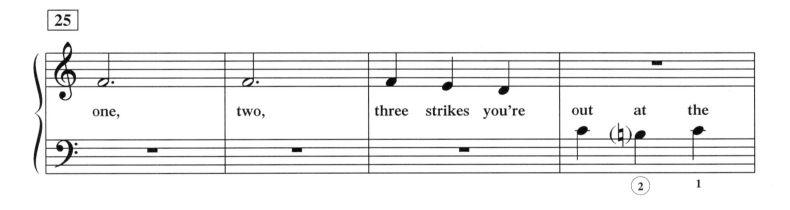

25

one,   two,   three strikes you're   out   at   the
②   1

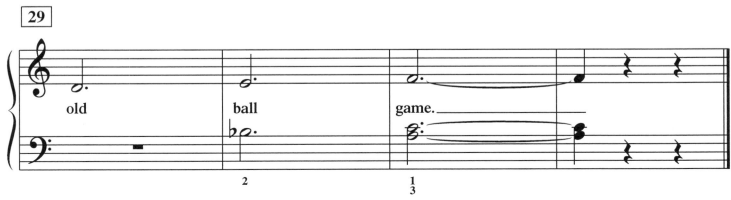

29

old   ball   game.
2   1
3

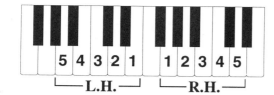

The Marionette's Funeral March

Secondo

Mysteriously
(Play both hands 1 octave lower)

Charles Gounod

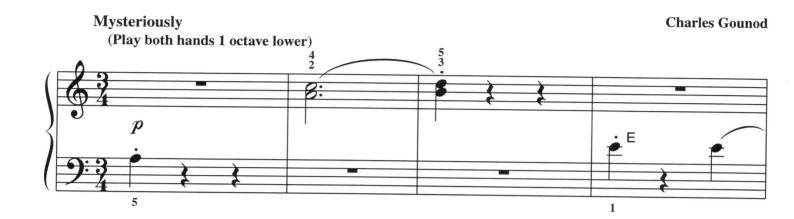

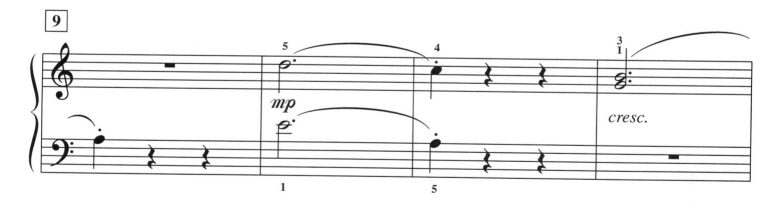

FF1145

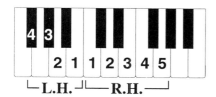

The Marionette's Funeral March

Primo

Charles Gounod

Mysteriously
(Play both hands 1 octave higher)

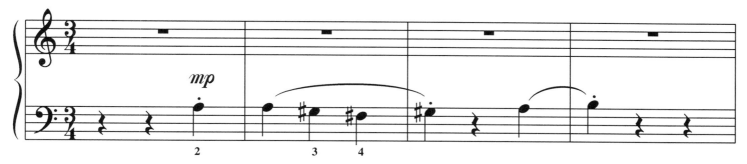

FF1145

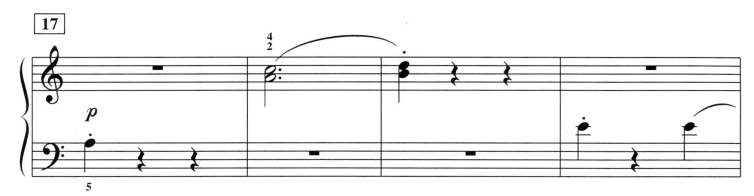

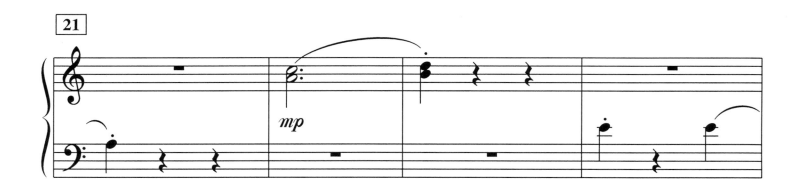

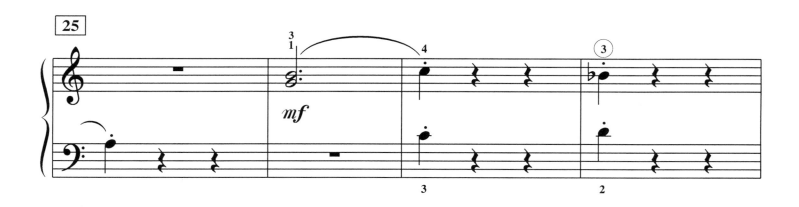

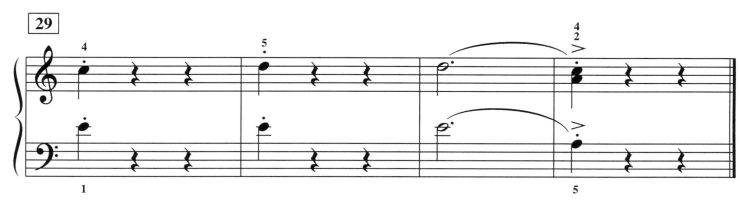

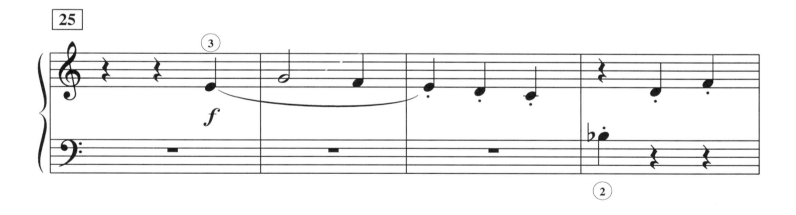

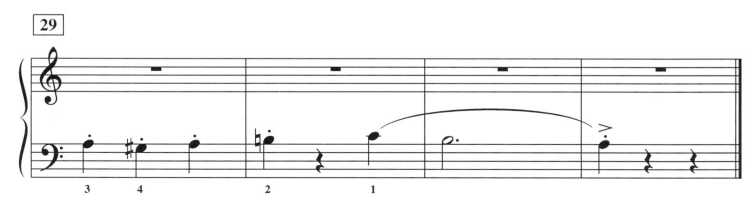

Dictionary of Musical Terms

$\dot{}$	*staccato*	Play the note short and detached.
$\overset{>}{}$	**accent**	Play an accented note louder, with emphasis.
(slur notes)	**slur**	Play these notes connected, smoothly.
rit.	*ritardando*	Slow down gradually.
$\frown$	*fermata*	Hold the note longer than usual.
♯	**sharp**	Raise the note by a half step.
♭	**flat**	Lower the note by a half step.
♮	**natural**	Cancels a sharp or flat.
	octave	A distance of 8 scale tones higher or lower. (Ex.: C up to C; F down to F.)
	Primo	The first part in a duet. Refers to the music for the player sitting on the right.
	Secondo	The second part in a duet. Refers to the music for the player sitting on the left.

Dynamic Symbols

p (*piano*) . . . . soft   *mf* (*mezzo-forte*) . . . . .medium loud

mp (*mezzo-piano*) . . . . .medium soft   *f* (*forte*) . . . . .loud

crescendo (*cresc.*) $\longleftarrow\!\!\!\!\!\!\!\!\!\!\!\longrightarrow$ $\longrightarrow\!\!\!\!\!\!\!\!\!\!\!\longleftarrow$ **diminuendo** (*dim.*)
play louder gradually   play softer gradually